SLA | GUIDELINES

Shelf Life,
Shelf Matters:
Managing Resources
in the School Library

Kathy Lemaire

Series Editor: Geoff Dubber

The School Library Association is an independent organisation and registered charity which was founded in 1937 to promote the development of libraries in schools. Today the SLA exists to support and encourage all those working in school libraries, raising awareness and promoting good practice through an effective training and publications programme. Membership of the Association brings many benefits including an advisory/information service for national and international enquiries, an excellent quarterly reviewing journal, and reduced rates for all publications and training courses. For full details, contact the SLA office in Swindon (address and telephone number below).

Acknowledgements

The author would like to thank Dianne Southcombe and Steve Hird for their helpful comments and suggestions, and Geoff Dubber and Marny Leech for their patience and support.

Published by the School Library Association
Unit 2, Lotmead Business Village
Lotmead Farm, Wanborough
Swindon SN4 0UY
Tel: +44 (0)1793 791787
Fax: +44 (0)1793 791786
email: publications@SLA.org.uk

© School Library Association, 2nd edn 2004

Printed by Will Print, Oxford

Contents

Introduction

Libraries have always been seen as essential to education, both formal and self-directed. In the Information Society of today they are even more important as the places where one can go to obtain information in all its forms, whether in books or in CD-ROMs, in archives or on the Internet. Effective school libraries, sometimes known as learning resource centres, provide essential material for supporting the curriculum, underpinning developing literacy and thinking skills, pursuing personal interests and, of course, reading for pleasure. They support teaching and learning throughout the school and satisfy the resource requirements of both staff and students.

However a library is only as good as the material it contains and the access it provides for its users. Efficient stock management is essential for effective resource provision, and this Guideline is intended to assist school library staff with its practical aspects. All library material will be covered, in paper or electronic formats, including items held within classroom book corners in primary and middle schools. Text books and reading scheme materials are excluded from the recommendations made here, though some of the criteria, for selection or discarding, for instance, might usefully be applied to this type of material as well.

The work of managing the library stock is on-going. There is never a point at which it is possible to say, 'The library is complete', only that the current phase of the work is finished. Stock management is also cyclical (see illustration below). When starting a new library, or developing an existing one, it is essential to start with policy creation and development planning and then continue the cycle. Generally, provided a good library policy and development plan are both in place, it is possible to start anywhere in this cycle, remembering to re-evaluate the development plan at the appropriate time.

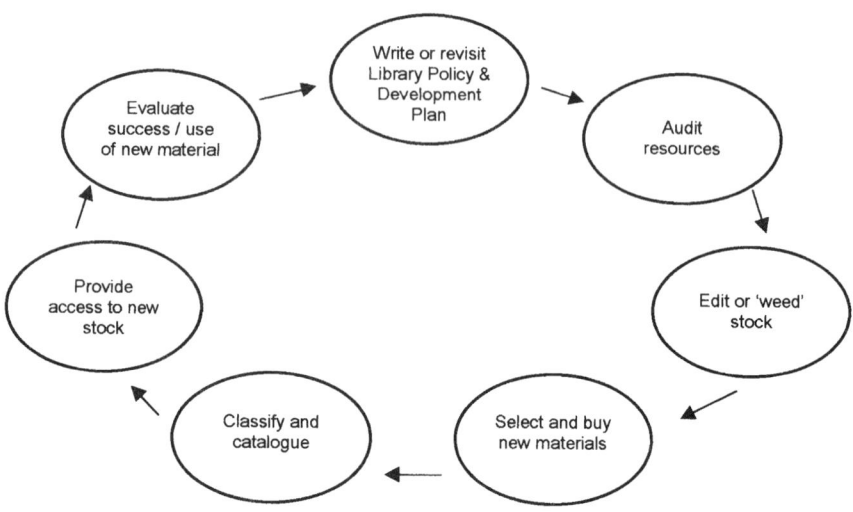

The stock management cycle in a school library

Policy statement

Every school library should have a policy statement, strongly rooted in the school mission statement and making clear the role of the library in fulfilling that mission. While it may be written by only one person, ideally it is created in a primary school by the staff exploring together what they need from the library, and in a middle or secondary school by a focus group. This may already be in place as a library committee, or may be created for this purpose. Any such group needs to contain at least one member of the school's senior management team (SMT) and preferably a governor.

The main purposes of such a document are to:

- make the role of the library within the school clear to staff, governors, inspectors and others
- provide a means of evaluating the service provided
- support budget bids for resourcing and staffing the library
- form the starting point for development planning.

The Library Policy needs to address such issues as accommodation, access to the library, selection and discarding of stock, services provided to students and teaching staff, and staffing of the library. It is a statement of what the library should be doing, and thus a basis for comparison with the current situation. For more details about developing a Library Policy, see the SLA Guidelines **Policy Making and Development Planning for the Primary School Library** and **Policy Making and Development Planning for the Secondary School LRC** (details on page 30).

Development plan

The Library Policy should lead to the creation of a Library Development Plan (LDP), which in turn should become part of the School Improvement Plan (SIP). So this too needs to be widely circulated and agreed by all the primary school staff; or submitted by a development group to the head teacher and SMT in a middle or secondary school.

'Library development planning maximises the educational benefits that derive from school libraries. Formulating a development plan specific to the library will:

1. help to ensure that the school addresses coherently both the library's central role in teaching and learning, and the need for it to secure resources to fulfil that role.
2. raise staff awareness of the library and promote thinking about teaching styles and learning strategies.
3. ensure the continuous improvement of library stock, services and use.' [1]

[1] Stewart Robertson, HMI, in SLA Guideline, **Development Planning for the School Library Resource Centre**, p. 4.

Content

The Library Development Plan needs to note the current provision, plan short- and long-term targets and objectives to fulfil the requirements of the Library Policy, and put into place methods of evaluating the level of success achieved. These will be specific to the needs of each school and created to meet particular requirements or gaps in provision. Examples of specific aims might be:

- to increase the fiction borrowing of 13-year-old boys

- to improve the science stock

- to introduce an 'Acceptable Use Internet Policy' [2]

- to create an out-of-hours Study Support Centre or Homework Club.[3]

Before the LDP can be written it is necessary to take a good look at the current provision of books and other material, in order to assess what improvement is needed (see next section). For more information on development planning, see **Policy Making and Development Planning for the Secondary School LRC** (details on page 30).

[2] see SLA Guideline, **Managing the Internet in the Primary and Secondary School Library**, p. 25.

[3] see **Open All Hours: Out of Hours Learning and the Secondary School LRC**, SLA Guideline, 2004.

Quick estimate

A good way of getting a quick estimate of current provision is to sample the book stock. To do this you can look at every tenth book in each classification section, until you have a sufficient number to give you a reasonable statistical sample. In a small section like the 100s, you may need to sample the whole collection; but in larger sections look at every tenth book until you have seen around fifty. For sections which are split into two or more subject areas, sample each subject. So for the 900s you should sample both the history and geography sections up to around fifty books in each. Do the same for the fiction collection, by sampling each alphabetical section until you have about twenty books from each. If your fiction collection is separated into different sequences for different age groups, then sample each of these.

For each book that you look at you should note:

- whether it is
  - a) less than two years old in that edition[4]
  - b) between two and ten years old
  - c) more than ten years old
- attractive and in good condition or battered and looking old-fashioned
- whether it has been borrowed in
  - a) the last year
  - b) the last five years
  - c) the last ten years
  - d) never, or not in the last ten years.

Similarly, all non-book materials such as CD-ROMs, cuttings files, maps, posters, videos, audiotapes, need to be assessed, but as there are far fewer of these, it is usual to assess each item individually.

Other collections

Primary schools should remember to assess any books held in the classroom for project work. Ideally, in secondary schools, material held in any satellite libraries belonging to departments should be assessed also. This is always a matter for tactful negotiation and in some schools it may not be possible.

Once this information has been gathered, it is easy to extrapolate percentages of stock which are likely to need replacing if the sample taken is a true reflection of the whole collection.

At the same time it is important to make a count of how many books there are in each non-fiction subject area, to ensure that the library stock supports

---

[4]   Obviously classic texts should not be rejected because of the date of first publication. However, the date of the current edition, either as a revised and updated edition (non-fiction) or in an attractive format with a modern looking cover (fiction) is an indicator of suitability and likely use in the school library.

the whole curriculum and not just some areas of it. A total for fiction books (but not reading scheme material) should also be calculated. Include any fiction held in classroom book corners, but sets of books used as class readers should not be included in this figure, as they are not available for individual use (except for the classes studying these texts).

Any items on long-term loan from your local School Library Service (SLS) [5] should be included in the sampling process and calculations of stock levels, as they are an integral part of your library resource provision. See Appendix 1 for an example of a data collection sheet for a stock audit.

At this point it is usually possible to get a clear idea of how much work needs to be done, and how much it will cost, to bring the library's resources up to the level required to actively achieve the purposes of the Library Policy.

Recommendations

The School Library Association recommends that the average number of items held should be in the range of 13 to 18 per pupil, in both primary and secondary schools; 15 would be a reasonable number to aim for, with 10 as an absolute minimum. The maximum number usually required would be around 20 per pupil, but these figures need to be adjusted for the size of school. So the smallest rural primary school should be resourced as if it had no less than 200 children, to allow each of them access to a good range of materials to suit their needs, interests and abilities: 200 x 15 books = 3000. A large secondary school will enjoy economies of scale, so the maximum stock required to meet all its students' needs effectively will be about 17,000 items. Any school with a sixth form will need to increase the provision for these students owing to the wide range of subjects taught; a sixth-form college may find that the requirement is more like 20 to 25 items per student.

The proportion of fiction to non-fiction in a primary school should normally be around 50:50; while in a middle or secondary school 65 to 75 per cent non-fiction and 25 to 35 per cent fiction is more usual. However, as more information is provided electronically these proportions are likely to change in favour of fiction.

Of course, a large stock does not necessarily equate with quality stock. All these items need to be up to date and attractive, with current information and appropriate access points (contents list, index, glossary). So a certain amount of stock editing will need to take place on a regular basis to weed out inappropriate and out-of-date material.

[5] In this publication, the term 'School Library Service (SLS)' refers to the resource and advisory services available from many local education authorities or public library services.

The purpose of stock editing, or weeding, is to remove the material that is no longer required, or suitable, for the stock of the school library. The only way to do this thoroughly is to examine each book or other item individually, to decide whether it should remain or not. If this has not been done for some time editing will remove large numbers of books from the shelves. This can be a little disturbing, and may need to be justified to other staff within the school. However, if the process is carried out in order to fulfil the purposes of the Library Policy and Development Plan, it can be demonstrated that this is a positive, planned activity, which will ultimately benefit the pupils. It is also demonstrably true that the 'leaner and fitter' library not only looks more attractive and visually welcoming but is of more use to the pupils than one which is padded out with irrelevant, out-of-date and unappealing stock.

Recommendations

The School Library Association recommends that the active life of a resource item is around ten years, although in subjects such as science, technology and geography – and with paperback fiction – replacement will need to be made after about five years. This recommendation is also made by HMI and by the Chartered Institute of Library and Information Professionals (CILIP). Therefore a school needs to make provision for the discarding and replacement of at least ten per cent of its book stock each year. If this has not been done for some time, a larger proportion of books will be in need of withdrawal.

Primary schools

In a primary school stock editing can be carried out in different ways. It can sometimes be done as a whole-staff activity on an INSET day. Each member of staff goes to the library and selects two or three books or other items which they feel should be withdrawn from stock. They then explain to their colleagues why this is so and a list of criteria is developed for weeding the sections. Everyone then works on a section, sometimes in pairs, and editing according to the agreed criteria. This is a good way for teachers to familiarise themselves with the materials in the library and gain 'ownership'.

If the school subscribes to the local School Library Service, it may be possible to pay for SLS staff to edit the library stock. In this case criteria should be agreed in advance so that the school knows what to expect from the work, and school library staff can also be involved. In primary schools this is particularly important as these teachers will often have closer links with their library and feel more ownership.

Alternatively, SLS staff will sometimes train up small teams of teachers, governors or teaching assistants (TAs) to use an agreed set of criteria. It is usually not a good idea to include parents in this activity as they have less knowledge of the curriculum and the range of abilities in the school. It can also be inhibiting for teaching staff to have parents observing the discarding of books which they have donated or raised funds for in the past. Discretion is needed here.

Middle and secondary schools

In a secondary school stock editing is usually the task of the school library staff, although in some schools each department sends one member of staff to assist with their subject area and an activity similar to that outlined above may then be appropriate. Middle schools might wish to use either of these models for developing editing criteria.

Criteria

It is often the case that the criteria for weeding resources have already been established as part of the Library Policy, and so everyone involved in the process is aware of these from the beginning. The School Library Association recommends that the following points should be considered when developing such criteria:

- non-fiction books and other information material must be relevant to the curriculum or students' leisure interests, and must contain current, accessible information with appropriate access points, such as index and bibliography

- fiction should contain good characterisation and storyline and enrich the reader with the quality of imagination and language used

- books must support individual private reading

- resources must be appropriate to the age and ability level of the whole school community

- resources need to be visually attractive to compete in the current world of the Internet, CD-ROMs, videos and DVDs

- resources must be free from bias, whether of gender, race, religion, politics or disability

- it is essential that all students are able to find books which reflect their own identity, especially in relation to culture and race. In primary schools especially, dual-language and mother-tongue material may be required, and in all schools resources reflecting the multicultural nature of today's society should be available.

Disposal

Disposal of the removed items can be a problem. Those that are in poor condition, or contain out-of-date or biased information, should be sealed into boxes and discarded or pulped. Second-hand book dealers will occasionally take old books that are in good condition, so it is sometimes worth asking them to take a look. Discarded fiction that is in good condition can be put into school sales or given to charity shops, as long as there is nothing offensive in the books (comments that could now be deemed racist or sexist, for example), provided they don't find their way back into school. Books to be donated to third world countries need to be assessed carefully, as much that is discarded here will not be of use anywhere else. It is often better to have a sale of suitable items and send the money instead.[6]

Cuttings files and posters, where these are maintained, are not usually weeded for age, but only for subjects that are no longer taught, as older material is still valid to show the development of ideas or conflicts.

Other non-book material also needs to go through a regular editing process. Software becomes outdated or corrupt; video and audio tapes may be damaged or the content no longer appropriate; and older technology, such as slides and filmstrips, may no longer be used in the school.

Historical items

Sometimes, if the library has not been edited for many years, interesting examples of books published in earlier decades come to light. In one LEA in the 1990s, many primary school libraries housed a book on rockets containing the phrase 'Some scientists believe that one day man will go to the moon'; while an inner city girls' school still had on its shelves books from the early years of the twentieth century with details of how to knit a vest or a bathing suit, or containing illustrations of students in gym-slips taking physical exercise by swinging clubs and marching. Clearly these are treasures to be preserved, and may be useful for history lessons. Such items can be the basis of a Heritage Collection. They should be clearly marked and not put back on the open shelves, but preserved elsewhere. Older material of local relevance may be precious and should also be preserved in a similar way. If items are particularly old or delicate it may be necessary to protect them with tissue paper and boxes made from acid-free materials.[7]

Other collections

Classroom collections in primary and middle schools should be included in this process. It is a good idea to bring all book corner material to the central library in order to assess it. Each class teacher can then choose a new selection from the resources remaining, and begin an exchange system which will allow circulation of books and other resources every term or every year, as desired.

---

[6] For further information about donating books or money, contact Book Aid International. Tel: 020 7733 3577; email: info@bookaid.org

[7] See **Setting the Scene: Local Studies Resources in the School Library**, for advice about storing old materials. SLA Guideline, 1999.

This will ensure much more effective management and use of resources. Ideally, departmental libraries in secondary schools should be part of this stock editing process. Many heads of department will be delighted for the library staff to work on their collections. The support of the head teacher or the SMT will help to ensure that these books are weeded to the same criteria as the library collections.

Prioritising

When the library stock has been thoroughly edited it is possible to assess the gaps in resourcing and begin active selection to meet the needs of the school as fully as possible. Selection should take account of any changes in the curriculum and the leisure needs of the students. If a large number of items has been weeded out, it may not be possible, or even desirable, to replace them all in the first year. Replacement over two or three years may need to be built into the Library Development Plan. Prioritising the expansion of sections of the library may also be necessary, especially if the school follows a two-year cycle in teaching some areas of the curriculum. There is little point in buying books immediately for a topic that will not be covered again until the year after next. Again, such priorities should be clear from the LDP.

As with editing, ideally teachers should be involved in the stock selection process. The library staff will need to consult regularly with teaching staff to ensure that appropriate curriculum support is provided and maintained. Teachers may request purchase of specific titles which they know about through their professional reading or subject associations.

Criteria for selection of new stock are likely to be similar to those adopted for editing purposes (see above). They should be already agreed and in the Library Development Plan.

Information about new resources

There are a variety of ways of finding out about new resources. With more than 8000 new titles for children and young people published every year in the UK alone, some shortcuts are needed to selecting the right ones. Reviewing journals, such as the *School Librarian, Carousel* and *Books for Keeps*, all provide a selection of excellent and reliable reviews (details on page 30). Some children's books are reviewed occasionally in *The Times Educational Supplement* and national newspapers. The *School Librarian* also contains a regular review section for websites and CD-ROMs.

Some school library services maintain an exhibition collection of recommended titles published in the last year or two, and may provide written reviews. Many organisations publish book lists on specific subjects relevant to their field of interest, and members of Young Book Trust[8] can also obtain useful book information and book lists. Recommendations can be invited from students about the books they would like to see in the library.

[8] at 45 East Hill, London SW18 2QZ and 137 Dundee Street, Edinburgh EH11 1BG.

A visit to the showroom of a library supplier specialising in children's books will provide a hands-on opportunity to examine the books, although there will be no pre-selection as in the methods mentioned above. It is also possible to use information from individual publishers, obtained from catalogues, websites or visits from publishers' reps. This is the least objective information about books and other resources and it is important not to be swayed by special offers, but to select only what you know you need for the library.

Sufficient funding

In order that the school library can be an effective provider of fiction and information material, sufficient funding needs to be available to allow managed development of the provision. A maintenance budget requires funding for replacement of at least ten per cent of the stock each year (see section on stock editing). Increased provision requires extra money.

The appropriate level of funding can be calculated by multiplying an average book price by the number of books to be purchased, and adding the cost of any non-book materials required, calculated in a similar way. Average book prices can be obtained from the Publishers Association or the local School Library Service, and are published in the *Bookseller*. Alternatively you can use the average cost of books bought for your school library in the last year. Find the mean average of the non-fiction bought, do the same for the fiction, and finally find the average of these two figures. This method avoids the final figure being skewed by a large number of low-cost paperbacks or expensive academic titles being bought in one year.

Recommendations

The School Library Association recommends that school managers provide sufficient funding for at least ten per cent of the library stock (including any held in classroom collections) to be replaced each year, with additional funding made available to bring the resources up to the recommended minimum levels (see page 6). Some of these resources, however, could be provided by short- and long-term loans from a School Library Service, a cost-effective way of increasing stock. A proportion of these loaned books can usually be exchanged regularly. Contact your local SLS for details of their full range of services.

Buying books

There are many places where school librarians and teachers can go to buy books. Library suppliers (see Appendix 3) provide large warehouse showrooms where it is possible to see a wide range of materials under one roof. These may be multiple-copy showrooms, where you take the items you want to buy and put them on a trolley. Alternatively, single-copy showrooms have only one copy of each title and you need to create a list of those you wish to order. While most of these books will be in stock, with this method it is always wise to order some extra titles as there are usually some that will be out of stock or even out of print. In both cases you will be told exactly how much you have spent at regular intervals, and after your visit you will be sent a printout of the titles selected.

Servicing

The advantage of buying from library suppliers is that they will do all the servicing,[9] or preparation, of your books if you wish, and deliver them ready to go on the shelves. If you use one of the main computerised library management systems, they can also provide you with records in the appropriate format to download on to your system, although you will have to add any keywords required. Discounts can be negotiated, and often the more you spend at any one time the greater the discount will be. Most library suppliers now also send out information about titles for selection purposes on CD-ROMs.

It is also possible to arrange discounts with local bookshops. These are best used for purchases of titles that you know you wish to buy, as they can stock only a small number of titles to select from and they will rarely provide any servicing of books. On-line booksellers such as <www.Amazon.co.uk>, on the other hand, provide you with a vast range of information which can equally make selection difficult; and they also will not provide servicing. Some school library services have a bookshop facility linked to their exhibition collection.

Buying from publishers' reps can be a useful way of selecting small numbers of books, but keeping appointments with reps from all the major publishers can be very time-consuming and you cannot make comparisons with similar titles from other publishers. It is rarely a good idea to buy remaindered books, however cheap they are, if the information in them could date. Check the date of publication before being tempted.

Acquisition record

Once you have obtained the new items, you need to make a record of them. This is known as an acquisition record. In the past, each item would be given a unique acquisition number and would be entered in an acquisition register. Nowadays most school librarians use their computer database for this purpose. Almost all middle and secondary schools, and an increasing number of primary schools, now use a purpose-built library management system to record their stock, provide a searchable database for student and staff access to the resources, and create records of loans. Most of these databases will automatically assign a unique identifying number, which can also be printed on a barcode attached to the item. For those schools without an ICT system, a card or paper-based record will be needed.

---

[9] Servicing can include covering, attaching spine labels, computer barcodes and date labels, or providing tickets to your specification. Library suppliers will also insert security tags and stamp the books with your school stamp. There is a small charge for this, but it saves large amounts of time for school library staff.

A catalogue record of each item is necessary in order to manage the library resources effectively and make them easier to find. Each record should contain several items of essential information:

- Title
- Author
- Publisher
- Date of publication
- Dewey class number or fiction (see next section)
- Date of purchase
- Type of media (book, video, CD-ROM, and so on).

In addition it is a good idea to include:

- at least one, and preferably several, suitable keywords that will help make searching for the item easier, and thus make it more accessible to both students and staff
- price
- location, if not in main library.

Computer record

Most secondary schools, and some middle and primary schools, now use a computer programme to record and circulate their resources. All of the major systems have a standard catalogue screen to complete when inputting material for the first time. It is necessary only to fill in as required. Examples are shown here from two systems, Alice from Softlink Europe and Heritage from IS Oxford.

Alice

Cataloguing: Management: Alice

Resource No. 1000002

Harry Potter et le prisonnier
The hobbit, or, There and back again / J.R.R. Tolkien
Horror Poetry

Accession

Title | The hobbit, or, There and back again
GMD | Text
Statement of responsibility | J.R.R. Tolkien
Author/Names | Tolkien J. R. R. John Ronald Revel
Edition | 4th ed
Additional edition | illustrated by the author
Publisher | Unwin Paperbacks; London
Publication year | 1981
Country of origin |
Series |
Physical description | 256p ill maps 18cm pbk
ISBN/ISSN | 0048231886   Control No. | B8100409

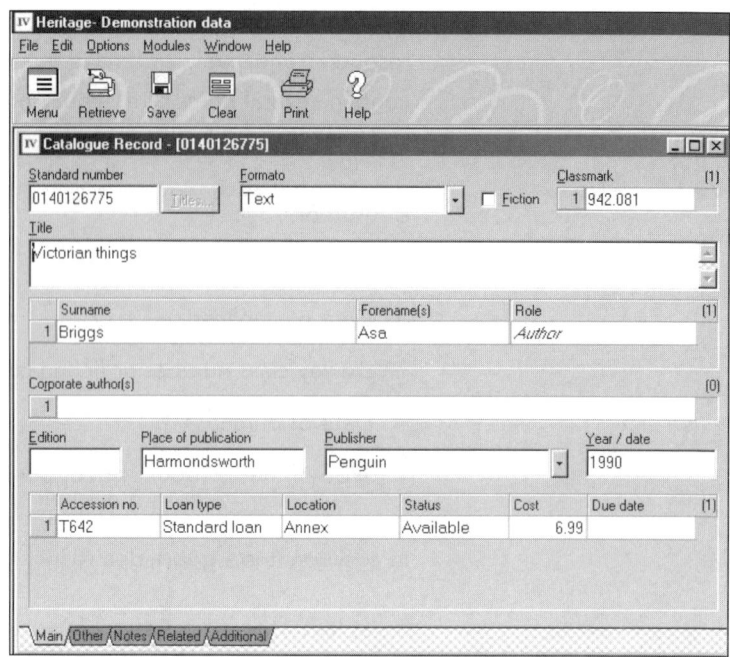

Card catalogue

If a computer is not used, then secondary schools may wish to consider developing, or restoring, a card catalogue. This will involve three sequences of catalogue cards; each non-fiction book will need an entry in all of them, while fiction books will need entries in two. A subject index will also need to be set up for the non-fiction; and preferably a keyword index for the fiction. A subject index is a comprehensive listing of subjects covered by the non-fiction items in the library, and the Dewey numbers where these items have been classified (see next section). Setting up and maintaining such a catalogue is very time consuming, and schools might be better advised to spend their time setting up a computer system. If this is not possible, the card sequences required are:

1. author entry (non-fiction and fiction titles)

2. title entry (non-fiction and fiction titles)

3. classified entry (non-fiction only).

For examples of these, and of keyword entries, see Appendix 2.

Management information

It is very difficult for the staff of a primary school to keep this type of card catalogue up to date and therefore of use. But it is important to ensure that information is available for two purposes: to provide information about items bought, for management purposes; and to provide access to the material for students and staff. If a primary school does not have a computer management system, information can be provided by making lists of new stock on a word processor or simple database, and making counts of older material not already listed. To enable access to the resources, it is possible to use a printed subject index. Subject indexes are produced by some school library services for use by their local primary schools, and items on loan from them will match their index. If there is not one available locally, a **Subject Index for Primary Schools** is an integral part of the School Library Association's **Primary School Classification Scheme** (see page 30). This has been created to be relevant to all countries of the British Isles and is licensed by OCLC Forest Press.

Wall chart

In addition to a comprehensive subject index, a simplified wall chart can be of use in primary schools to enable children to find the most popular subjects quickly, and to help them to understand the relationship between Dewey numbers and the order of books. Some primary schools create a new one each term, covering the topics they will be teaching.

Classification

Dewey System

In order to make it possible to find items when they are required, it is necessary to arrange them in a logical order. In most school libraries they will be organised in a numerical system called the Dewey Decimal Classification scheme (DDC). This is also used in the majority of public and university libraries, so a pupil who has learned to use the scheme in school will be able to transfer this skill to other libraries. DDC has been in use for well over a hundred years and has been revised regularly to take account of new branches of knowledge and new subjects that need to be classified.

All subjects are divided up into ten classes, which are numbered from 000 to 900. Each class is then broken down individually to provide more specific numbers from 001 to 999. Finally decimal places are used to add further distinction within subjects.

It is usual for schools to use a truncated version of DDC as some of the numbers can be very long. Classifying with numbers of up to two decimal places is suitable for middle and secondary schools, and in primary schools it should not be necessary to use numbers after the decimal point in more than a few cases; for history books, for example, where it is necessary to separate different chronological periods for the same country. Infant schools will not usually need any decimal places at all.

Colour coding

Some primary schools may wish to use a colour coding system on their books. However, as there is only a small number of colours that can be used, this cannot be specific but is only a very general guide to the shelf where a book is likely to be found, or where it should be reshelved. It is impossible, using colour coding alone, to bring all books on a specific subject (football, for example, or the geography of Ireland, or the Victorians) together on one shelf. If a colour coding scheme is used, it should be in conjunction with a simplified Dewey scheme, to aid pupils in finding the general sections. Experience shows that children, even at infant level, can handle the Dewey system in a simple form, and that it will help reinforce numeracy skills.

There is at present no secondary school version of DDC available. The School Library Association published a primary version suitable for use in Scotland, Wales, Ireland and England in 2001.[10] This also provides instructions on how to classify books. The full Dewey scheme and the abridged version are available from OCLC Europe.[11]

---

[10] **Primary School Classification Scheme** containing two booklets: the **Subject Index** and a **Practical Guide** to the scheme; a CD-ROM and a poster (full details on page 30).

[11] OCLC Europe, 7th Floor, Tricorn House, 51–53 Hagley Road, Birmingham B16 8TP. Tel: 0121 456 4656.

Once a catalogue has been set up in the school library, a stock check should be carried out annually. This will require the library to be closed for about a week, and so in a secondary school it is usually undertaken out of school time. In many school libraries the time chosen is at the end of the summer term, either before or after the school has broken up. It might be possible to arrange for the local School Library Service to carry out the annual stock check.

Missing items

As well as assessing the library resources for condition and use, each item is checked against its catalogue record, to identify those items that are missing. Many computerised library management systems make this a relatively easy activity to carry out, and it can often be done with a hand-held data capture unit. With a manual catalogue, it is necessary to check each resource against it, and any items not found must be checked against the record of those out on loan before marking them as missing. The catalogue cards for any lost items must then be removed from every sequence. In a secondary school, if there are serious losses, it may be necessary to consider installing a security system.

It is always a good idea, however, to declare an 'amnesty' in school before carrying out a stock check. Dump bins can be placed around the school so that students can anonymously return items that are long overdue or where the loan was never recorded. Loss of any fines in such instances are normally more than offset by the value of the returned items.

Overdue loans

During the school year, reminders of overdue items should be sent out on a regular basis, and while the first one is usually to the pupil (except in the case of the youngest children), the second reminder is often addressed to the class teacher or form tutor. Many schools send final overdue notices, including the cost of the item, to the parents. Withdrawal of library privileges is occasionally used as a final sanction for persistent offenders, although many schools believe that this is not the right solution. Similarly, some secondary schools do not charge fines for overdue books, as this may disadvantage some children and make them less likely to return items. Primary schools almost never charge fines.

If a primary school has lists of only the more recent books, then only these can be stock checked. However, it is still possible to monitor any issue system to ensure books are returned, and to make a count of library items to make sure that the school is not losing valuable resources in large quantities.

Resources on loan from a School Library Service should be included in any stock check.

Shelving

The majority of library resources are books, which require appropriate shelving to contain and protect them and make them available to students and staff. Books are shelved from left to right and down each bay of shelves, before starting at the top of the next bay. They are also normally shelved in a logical sequence around the room in order of class number for non-fiction, alphabetical order of author's name for fiction, and with a separate section for reference-only material. It is important to follow these conventions for several reasons, but principally because this is how all other libraries will shelve their books, and it is important that users learn and understand this.

Adjustable shelving

As books are not all the same size, and as you may wish to move sections of the stock to new locations, it is important that the shelving is adjustable. It is also essential to ensure that the shelving you choose has integral bookstops or supports as part of the system, to avoid books falling over and sliding off the shelf. This type of shelving is usually made of metal, and comes in a variety of colours. It can also have end panels attached if required, for posters or general display. Shelving systems of this nature will allow for interchangeable display shelves and storage facilities for runs of periodicals to be incorporated. Shelves of different widths are available for fiction and non-fiction books, but picture books are best kept in kinderboxes – low wooden boxes on legs with divisions to allow several runs of picture books to be contained, front cover out. These books are not normally in any order, but can be browsed freely by the youngest children.

Recommendations

It is important not to have the shelving too high, so that the youngest pupil in the school can reach the top shelves without too much trouble. The usual recommendation is a maximum height of:

- 1200 mm for primary schools

- 1500 mm for middle schools

- 1800 mm for secondary schools.

It is also better not to have shelving too low as evidence shows that borrowing rates of books located near the floor are low.

Special schools with students who have physical difficulties, such as the need for a wheelchair, will have to adjust their shelves to suit their users.

Labels indicating where particular subjects are kept – called guiding – should be attached to the shelves. As the stock may be moved around the shelves, depending on curriculum need and what is on loan, it is important that the guiding is not fixed. A slot at the front of the shelving is ideal for this.

Health and safety

Safety is an important factor in deciding which shelves to use. A bay of shelving full of books is very heavy, so DIY shelving is rarely adequate and is often dangerous. Buy shelving which has been designed for the purpose, and ensure it is fixed to the wall if this is what is intended by the manufacturer. (See Appendix 3 for a list of suppliers.)

Non-book material

Storage for non-book material is also available from shelving suppliers, and can range from expensive cabinets to vinyl wallets suspended from metal holders. Make sure that it is possible to label items adequately, and display them for selection when required.

Security

A well-equipped school library is a very valuable resource. The replacement cost for all the items in it will be many thousands of pounds. Although loss from fire, flood or other disaster cannot be avoided, it is possible to minimise losses due to stealing.

Minimising losses

There are many ways of achieving this. CD-ROMs can be protected by using a 'jukebox' system and networking them, so that students do not handle the originals. Computers and peripherals can be indelibly marked and physically constrained. The items that 'walk' most regularly, however, are books. Many middle and secondary schools now minimise these losses by using specialist library security systems, and occasionally by installing video surveillance equipment, if it is in use elsewhere in the school.

Library security systems rely on a tag inserted in the book in a place where it is difficult for potential thieves to find it – usually down the spine, under the barcode label, or between two pages close to the spine of the book. These tags are initially inserted in the existing stock, but if new books are serviced by a library supplier they will insert tags for you. Some people only insert tags in expensive books, but it is probably better to use the system in every book if it is in use at all. The main cost in such systems is in the security gates, so to tag only a portion of the stock is a false economy. It is also unwise to allow students, however trustworthy, to assist with this procedure, as the location of the tags will soon become common knowledge within the school.

The tags are activated so that they will sound an alarm when passed through security gates. Some systems rely on the tags being de-activated when the item is loaned, while others remain activated and the items are passed around the security gate by staff. The latter system can pose a problem for students, however, as these items occasionally trigger alarms in shops or in the public library.

Schools which have invested in a security system have shown that such a system, while expensive initially, can dramatically reduce losses and pay for itself in a relatively short time. A general rule of thumb is that if the cost of installing a system is less than the value of items lost over five years, it is worth installing. The value of missing books can be estimated during the annual stock check (see page 19).

Primary schools

Most primary schools are unlikely to find a security system of benefit, as their libraries are rarely staffed continuously, and in any case they are less likely to have a real problem with theft.

For details of suppliers of some of these systems, see Appendix 3.

Once the library is ready, it is important that staff and students are taught how to use it. If major changes have been made, the whole school community must learn how an issue system works, for example, or how to use the new catalogue. Guided tours and printed handouts will help, but each class will need its first session in the revamped or new library to be one of exploration and discovery. If only minor changes have taken place, they can be incorporated into an on-going information skills programme. New students and staff will need induction sessions in the library. The SLA Guidelines series includes titles giving advice on library induction and on developing information skills.

Grand opening

It is often a good exercise in raising the library profile to have a grand opening of a new or revamped library. This can be the highlight of a book week, with visiting authors and storytellers. Some schools take the opportunity of making a video, showing the before and after scenes, as well as what happened in between. At this point it is important to stop and catch your breath and give yourself a pat on the back for what you have achieved. Well-earned praise can be given to all those who have helped, before the whole stock management cycle begins again.

Appendix 1:
Data Collection Sheet for a Superficial Stock Audit in a School Library

Use for sampling all class sections and alphabetical sections of fiction books.

Fill in using 'five bar gates'.

Dewey No. or Fiction Letter	Number looked at	Number shabby	Older than 10 years	2 to 10 years old	Newer than 2 years	Borrowed in last 2 years	Never borrowed

1: **author entry card**, to be filed in alphabetical order of author's last name (non-fiction and fiction examples shown)

GRAHAM, IAN 070
   Books and newspapers
Evans, 2000
	COLFER, EOIN FIC
	   The wish list
	O'Brien Press, 2000

2: **title entry card**, to be filed in alphabetical order of first word of title, ignoring words like 'the' and 'a' (non-fiction and fiction examples shown)

BOOKS AND NEWSPAPERS 070
   Graham, Ian
Evans, 2000
	THE WISH LIST FIC
	   Colfer, Eoin
	O'Brien Press, 2000

3: **subject entry card**, to be filed in numerical order (non-fiction only)

PUBLISHING 070
   GRAHAM, IAN
      Books and newspapers
Evans, 2000

4: **keyword entry card**, to be filed alphabetically by subject (optional – fiction only)

FANTASY FIC
   COLFER, EOIN
      The wish list
O'Brien Press, 2000

Appendix 3:
Library Suppliers

Books and other resources

Askews Library Services
218–222 North Road
Preston PR1 1SY
Tel: 01772 555947
Fax: 01772 254860
email: mail@askews.co.uk

Books for Students
Bird Road
Heathcote
Warwick CV34 6TB
Tel: 01926 436436
email: info@bfs.co.uk

Cypher Group
(previously Morley Books & JMLS)
Elmfield Road
Morley
Leeds LS27 0NN
Tel: 01132 012900
Fax: 01132 012929

Heath Educational Books
Willow House
off Whittaker Road
Sutton
Surrey SM3 9QQ
Tel: 020 8644 7788
Fax: 020 8641 3377

Peters Bookselling Services
120 Bromsgrove Street
Birmingham B5 6RL
Tel: 0121 666 6646
email: sales@peters-books.co.uk

Woodfield & Stanley Ltd
Broad Lane
Moldgreen
Huddersfield HD5 8DD
Tel: 01484 421467
email: info@woodfield-stanley.co.uk

Library stationery, shelving and equipment

Amenco Library Systems
Willis Way
Poole
Dorset BH15 3ST
Tel: 01202 676011
Fax: 01202 671436
email: office@amenco.co.uk

Finnmade Furniture Ltd
Lynton House
6 Newlands Lane
Hitchin SG4 9AY
Tel: 01462 452001
Fax: 01462 452002

Don Gresswell Ltd
(part of DEMCO Worldwide Ltd)
Grange House
2 Geddings Road
Hoddesdon
Hertfordshire EN11 0NT
Tel: 01992 454500
Fax: 01992 448300
email: direct@gresswell.co.uk

LFC
(part of DEMCO Worldwide Ltd)
Phoenix House
54 Denington Road
Wellingborough NN8 2QH
Tel: 01933 442777
Fax: 01933 229925
email: despatchline@lfc-ltd.co.uk

Librex
Colwick Road
Nottingham NG2 4BG
Tel: 0115 950 4664
Fax: 0115 958 6683
email   sales@librex.co.uk

Point Eight Ltd
Shaw Road
Dudley
West Midlands DY2 8TP
Tel: 01384 238282
email: sales@point8.co.uk

Security systems

3M Library Systems
Customer Technical Centre
Easthampstead Road
Bracknell RG12 1JE
Tel: 01344 866485
Fax: 01344 866495
email: library-uk@mmm.com

Plescon Security Products
Unit 9, Sterling Complex
Sproughton Business Park
Farthing Road
Ipswich IP1 5AP
Tel: 01473 747159
Fax: 01473 747252
email: info@plescon.co.uk

Sensormatic Ltd
Harefield Grove
Rickmansworth Road
Harefield
Uxbridge UB9 6JY
Tel: 01895 873795

Appendix 4:
Care and Repair of Books

An attractive, clean and cared-for book is much more likely to encourage children to pick it up and to take care of it themselves. It is always worthwhile putting some time and effort into this. Volunteer parents and students can be used for this chore, as it gives a feeling of pride and ownership to transform a book and return it to circulation.

When returned books are being put back on the shelves, they should always be quickly assessed for condition. Any that are vandalised, badly damaged or falling apart need to be disposed of, but not before a note has been made of the title and author so that a replacement can be bought. A newer edition, or even an alternative title, may need to be purchased. Fiction can often be bought with a more modern cover, and increasingly hardback fiction is giving way to paperback, which students prefer both to read and to carry.

The record of a discarded item will need to be removed from any catalogue, whether manual (such as card catalogue), or computerised.

Books that are not badly damaged, or are dirty, can be repaired or cleaned and put back into circulation.

Plastic jackets

Plastic jackets are used to cover and protect the publishers' paper jacket on a hardback book. They should be cleaned, if looking a little grubby, with a cloth dampened with a weak solution of washing-up liquid. Some marks may require white spirit, and there is now a patent book cleaning fluid which you may wish to use. Be careful to store these fluids safely and out of the reach of children. Make sure that the books are dry before they are put back on the shelf, as otherwise they will stick together and they may become smelly.

Damaged or worn plastic jackets should be replaced with new ones. Be careful how you attach these to the book, so that they do not tear an attractive endpaper when they are replaced. Spine labels should also be replaced. Be careful to ensure that they are covered with a badge protector or Scotch 'Magic Tape'. It is important not to use ordinary transparent tape as this will go yellow and fall off, leaving a nasty residue.

Pages

Books that have pages missing should be disposed of, as they will be of no use to students.

If the pages are not too badly torn it is possible to repair them with Scotch 'Magic Tape'. This matt tape, while looking opaque on the roll, will disappear on the page and is much more suitable for repair of pages than other types of shiny sticky tape. If there are a lot of damaged pages in a book, it is better to replace it.

Grubby pages can sometimes be transformed by cleaning them with a clean white eraser, while a small indelible scribble can be Tippexed out.

Covers

If the covers have come away from a hardback book, and the rest of the book is still up to date and in good condition, it is possible to stick them back, but it is not an easy job to make the book look good.

1. First coat the exposed bound spine with a strong paper adhesive.

2. Lay the book in the correct position with the outer cover facing down and tape the front cover to the front endpaper with a strong, sticky-backed linen tape.

3. Turn the book to the back and tape this cover in place also, ensuring that you keep the spine against the cover, so that the adhesive will hold.

4. Finally, close the book and bind tightly with strong elastic bands or string, to ensure that it remains in this position until the adhesive has dried (for a few days will be best).

It is always a good idea, particularly with primary children, to spend some time teaching them to value and take care of books. Points to be mentioned include:

- always wash hands before using a book

- never leave it on the floor to be trodden on

- never use foreign objects as bookmarks

- always close the book and return it to the shelf or kinderbox when finished with it

- never allow babies to chew books.

Adult role models are particularly important in encouraging this sort of behaviour.

Other Sources of Information

Journals

School Librarian Unit 2, Lotmead Business Village, Lotmead Farm, Wanborough, Swindon SN4 0UY
Membership of the School Library Association includes a subscription to the *School Librarian* which is packed with interesting articles and age-ranged reviews of books as well as CD-ROMs and websites.

Books for Keeps 6 Brightfield Road, Lee, London SE12 8QF
A very lively bi-monthly magazine that should be in every primary school library; full of articles, author information, news about books, and book reviews.

BOOX Well Worth Reading, 3 Norman Road, Winchester SO23 9PW
A wacky magazine aimed at 13 to 19-year-olds, full of comment, information and book suggestions from librarians, celebrities and young readers themselves.

Carousel 7 Carrs Lane, Birmingham B4 7TG
Magazine of the Federation of Children's Book Groups. Comes out three times a year (March, June, October) and flags up the best of the new children's books.

Organisations

Children's Books Ireland 19 Parnell Square, Dublin 1
Publishes a journal biannually *Inis*.

Young Book Trust 45 East Hill, London SW18 2QZ and 137 Dundee Street, Edinburgh EH11 1BG
Look out for the annual ***100 Best Books*** publication. Also, subscription to Young Book Trust entitles you to theme or age-related book lists on request.
www.booktrusted.co.uk

SLA Guidelines

Developing Information Literacy Skills Through the Primary School Library. 1999. 0 900641 95 9

Issue Systems for the Primary School Library. 1998. 0 900641 89 4

Open All Hours: Out of Hours Learning and the Secondary School LRC. 2004. 1 903446 23 6

Policy Making and Development Planning for the Primary School Library. 2001. 1 903446 10 4

Policy Making and Development Planning for the Secondary School LRC. 2003. 1 903446 22 8

Setting the Scene: Local Studies Resources in the School Library. 1999. 0 900641 92 4

Primary School Classification

Primary School Classification Scheme
Pack containing **Practical Guide**. 1 903446 02 3. **Subject Index**. 1 903446 01 5. CD-ROM (containing SubjectSearch, a simple database, as well as the text of the two booklets). 1 903446 03 1. A3 Poster.

CALDERDALE LIBRARIES